IT'S TIME TO EAT BROCCOLI

It's Time to Eat Broccoli

Walter the Educator

Silent King Books
A WhichHead Entertainment Imprint

Disclaimer

This book is a literary work; the story is not about specific persons, locations, situations, and/or circumstances unless mentioned in a historical context. Any resemblance to real persons, locations, situations, and/or circumstances is coincidental. This book is for entertainment and informational purposes only. The author and publisher offer this information without warranties expressed or implied. No matter the grounds, neither the author nor the publisher will be accountable for any losses, injuries, or other damages caused by the reader's use of this book. The use of this book acknowledges an understanding and acceptance of this disclaimer.

It's Time to Eat Broccoli is a collectible early learning book by Walter the Educator suitable for all ages belonging to Walter the Educator's Time to Eat Book Series. Collect more books at WaltertheEducator.com

USE THE EXTRA SPACE TO TAKE NOTES AND DOCUMENT YOUR MEMORIES

BROCCOLI

It's time to eat broccoli, little and green,

It's Time to Eat
Broccoli

The tiniest trees that you've ever seen!

With florets so fluffy and stems that stand tall,

This veggie's a hero, both big and small.

It grows in the garden, in sunshine so bright,

With rain drops and cool air, it grows just right.

The farmers all tend it, with care and delight,

'Til it's ready for us on our plates at night!

Let's munch on each bite, give it a try,

Broccoli's tasty, don't be shy!

It's crunchy and crispy, with flavor so bold,

A treasure of vitamins, or so we're told.

Inside every stalk and every green top,

Are tiny, strong nutrients that don't stop!

There's Vitamin C to keep us all strong,

And fibers to help us move right along.

It's Time to Eat

Broccoli

So let's munch together, chew and repeat,

Broccoli's the best little green treat!

With each bite we grow big, strong, and spry

Broccoli, broccoli, give it a try!

It's Time to Eat

Broccoli

ABOUT THE CREATOR

Walter the Educator is one of the pseudonyms for Walter Anderson. Formally educated in Chemistry, Business, and Education, he is an educator, an author, a diverse entrepreneur, and he is the son of a disabled war veteran. "Walter the Educator" shares his time between educating and creating. He holds interests and owns several creative projects that entertain, enlighten, enhance, and educate, hoping to inspire and motivate you. Follow, find new works, and stay up to date with Walter the Educator™

at WaltertheEducator.com